ABC
Letters

D1469574

By Lillian Lieberman
Illustrated by Corbin Hillam

Publisher: Roberta Suid
Editor: Elizabeth Russell
Cover Design: David Hale
Design and Production: Mary Francis

ISBN 0-912107-10-3

Printed in the United States of America

9 8 7 6 5

INTRODUCTION

ABC LETTERS provides worksheets, bulletin boards, and a game to reinforce the learning of the alphabet for preschool, kindergarten, and primary children. Reproducible worksheets encourage the identification and discrimination of each alphabet letter through coloring, cutting, pasting, circling, drawing, and playing simple games. Each activity contains words and pictures which begin with the letter to be learned. Each page also contains a self-check, such as a path to follow or complete, a picture to discover, a letter to find among a set of letters. The imaginative content of each activity is designed to stimulate the young child's interest in mastering the alphabet.

All upper and lower case manuscript letters are taught in *ABC LETTERS.* The upper and lower case forms of each letter are printed at the top of each page of Section I for easy student reference. Directional arrows help the child to trace the letters in correct sequence. The child traces and names the letter at the same time.

In addition to worksheets, *ABC LETTERS* includes directions and full set-ups for file-folder games. These games, for two or more children, may be used for free time activities or as extra reinforcement. For more active class participation, *ABC LETTERS* provides hands-on bulletin board ideas for teachers to create. Children use these displays to match upper case letters to proper nouns and to sort lower case letters into containers.

Through a variety of activities, *ABC LETTERS* introduces the learning of the alphabet as an initial step toward reading, writing, and spelling. Special education teachers may find the activities useful to meet the needs of their students. The activities can also be taken home for assignments and for sharing with those at home.

A special feature of this activity book is the use of the multi-sensory approach to learning. The child names and traces the letters for auditory-kinesthetic support. Tracing upper and lower case letters emphasizes letter-size relationships. Association of alphabet letters with words comes from visual picture support. Tracing, circling, cutting, pasting, and coloring develop fine motor skills. The child learns letters through sight, sound, and movement.

Directions for Worksheets

Part I: Upper and lower case association
1. Children name each letter as they trace its dotted pattern. For example, "upper case A, lower case a."
2. Children cut out the upper case picture parts at the bottom of the page. Have them paste these pictures to the matching lower case picture parts at the top of the page for letter association. Be sure students match the two halves of a picture correctly according to size, shape, or pattern.
3. You may wish to have children color the pictures.

Part II: Lower case letter activities
1. Children name each lower case letter as they trace its dotted pattern at the top of the page.
2. Explain specific directions for each page, such as cut, paste, color, or fold. Then have children carry out directions.

Enrichment Activities

1. **Feely Letters** Cover large letter cut-outs with textured material such as corduroy or sandpaper. Place these in a box in which you have cut a round hole large enough for a child's hand. Glue the ribbing of a sock to this hole to keep students from seeing inside the box. The child slips a hand into the box and feels one of the letters. He or she names the letter, then takes it out of the box to check. If correct, the student gets another turn.

2. **Treasure Hunt** Place capital letters around the classroom in plain view. Have children close their eyes and put their heads down on their desks. Place a lower case letter on each desk. Ask children to look at the letter, name it, and find its capital mate. If correct, the child gets to place the capital letter in another part of the room and returns the lower case letter for use in another round of play. This game can be played in reverse, with children hunting for lower case letters.

3. **Seven Letters** Select seven children to come to the front of the room. Have the rest of the class put heads down on desks with eyes closed. Hand each of the seven children two identical letters. These children tiptoe around the room, placing one of their letters on another child's desk. The seven return to the front with their letters behind their backs. Seated children who have received a letter ask one of the seven if he or she has their letter. A correct guess earns a turn as one of the seven up.

4. **Letter Carnival** Have children bring in pictures or small objects to which you tape a card telling the letter with which the word begins. Give children five different letter cards. Have small groups of children take turns "buying" objects which begin with the same letters as their cards. To buy an object, a child must correctly name its letter. One child becomes the "cashier" and collects the cards. Children may share what they bought at the end of play for further language experience. Recycle the objects for another round of play.

Pick A Letter

Objective:
To develop perception and discrimination of lower case letters

Materials:
Colored construction paper, straight pins

Construction:
1. Cut out a tree, grass, 3 baskets, and at least 24 apples from construction paper.
2. Staple the tree, grass, and the title "Pick a Letter" to bulletin board.
3. Select 3 lower case letters for children to master. Write letters on apples with felt pen. Punch a hole at top of each apple and hang on the bulletin board with straight pin.
4. Label each basket with a letter to be learned. Staple baskets to bulletin board, then stick 8-10 pins in each basket.

Procedure:
1. Each child picks an apple from the tree, names the letter, and places it on a pin in the correct basket.
2. When all apples have been picked, put them back on the tree to be used again.
3. Place new sets of letters on the bulletin board after children master old ones. Use other fruits, leaves, nuts, or even lollipops on the tree. Note the kinesthetic support given through the manipulation and naming of letters.

Capital Round-Up

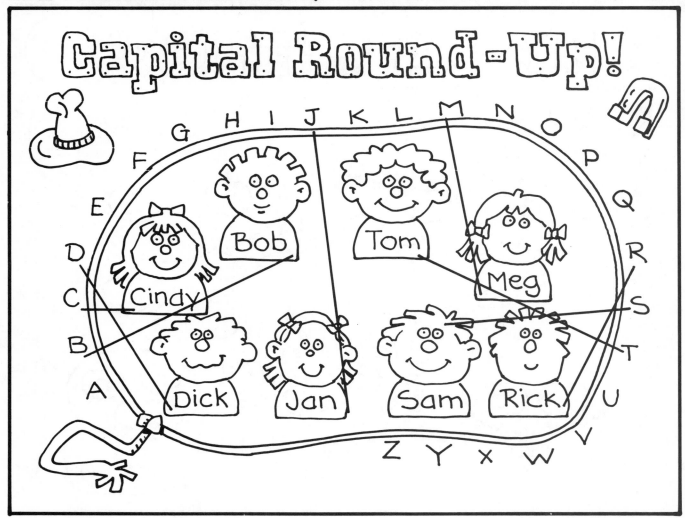

Objective:
To reinforce recognition of upper case letters

Materials:
Colored construction paper, crayons or paints, yarn, glue, straight pins

Construction:
1. Cut out and distribute head shapes.
2. Have students make self-portraits using crayons or paints, gluing on yarn for hair.
3. Write each child's name on portrait.
4. Staple pictures to bulletin board. Encircle the portraits with a yarn lasso. Pin bulletin board capital letters in order around the lasso.

5. Attach a length of yarn with a loop at free end to first letter of each name.
6. You may wish to add paper cut-outs of a cowboy hat and a horseshoe to the bulletin board.

Procedure:
1. Each child names the letter with which his or her name begins and matches it to the capital letter on the bulletin board by looping the yarn over its pin.
2. Use the same bulletin board arrangement to emphasize capital letters in the name of streets and cities, days of the week, months of the year, states, and abbreviations.

6

Alphabet Match Game

Objective:
To identify and associate upper and lower case letters

Materials:
Oak tag or card stock, file folder, large envelope

Construction:
1. Duplicate game board and card pages.
2. Glue game board inside file folder, cards to oak tag or card stock.
3. Laminate all pieces, if desired.
4. Attach envelope to back of folder for storing cards.

Procedure:
1. This is a game for two players. One player shuffles the lower case cards and deals 13 to each person. Players place cards face up in the top row of their side of game board. Dealer shuffles the upper case cards and places them face down on the fish.
2. Each player in turn takes a card from the fish pile. If there is a match, the player places it in the bottom row of the game board. If it is unmatched or incorrectly named or matched, the card goes into the square discard pile.
3. Play continues until one player fills up all the letter spaces with matched letters. If all of the fish pile cards are used before this happens, the discard pile is placed face down on the fish and play resumes until cards are gone.
4. The game can be played several times. The upper case letter can be placed first, with the game emphasis on the lower case match.

Upper Case Letters

A	B	C	D	E
F	G	H	I	J
K	L	M	N	O
P	Q	R	S	T
U	V	W	X	Y
Z				

Lower Case Letters

a	b	c	d	e
f	g	h	i	j
k	l	m	n	o
p	q	r	s	t
u	v	w	x	y
z				

DISCARD
PILE

FISH

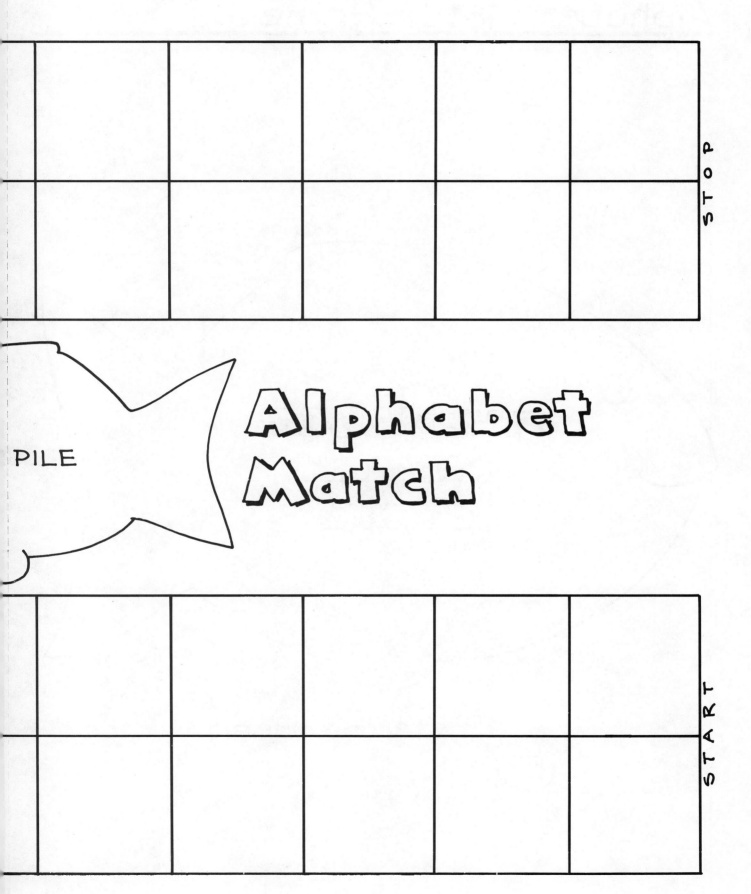

STOP

PILE

Alphabet Match

START

Alphabet Match Game

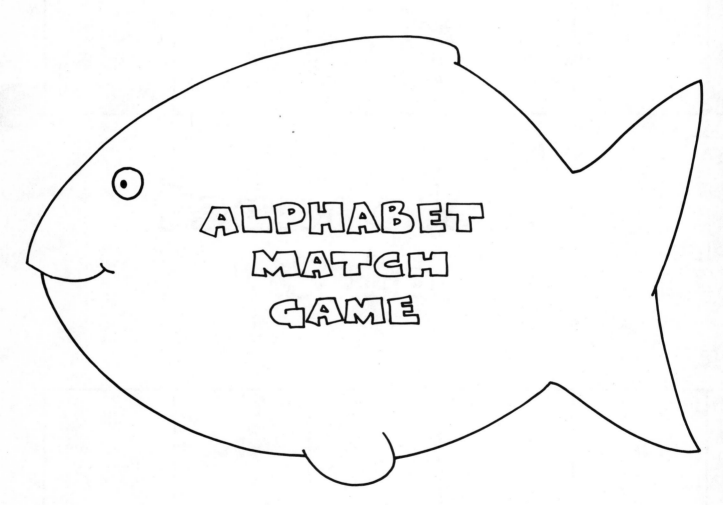

Paste on folder.

Aa

Name

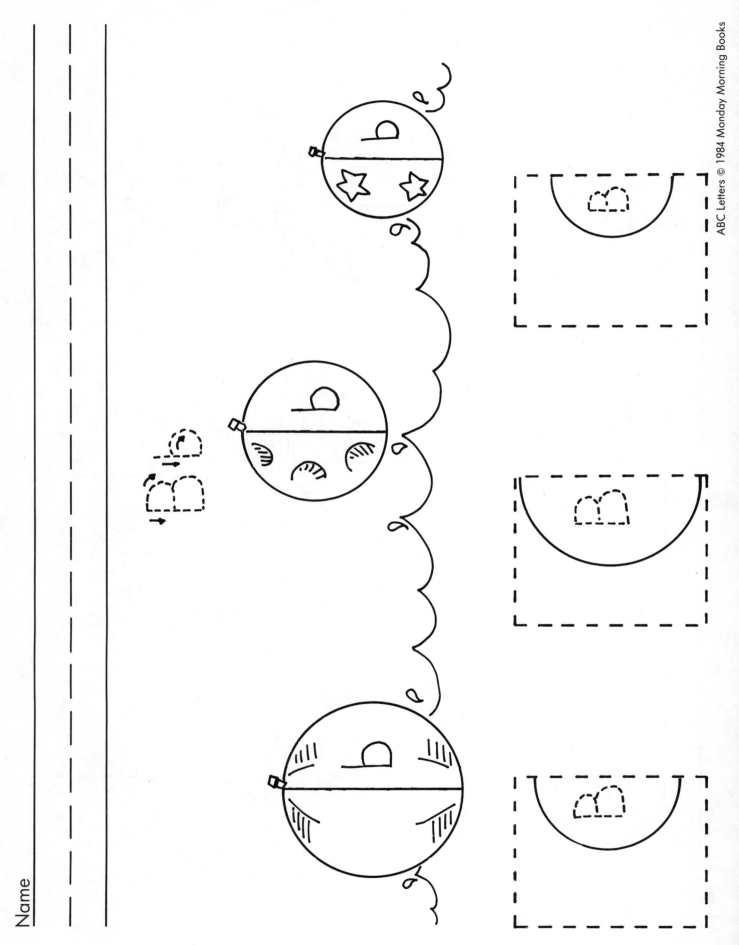

ABC Letters © 1984 Monday Morning Books

15

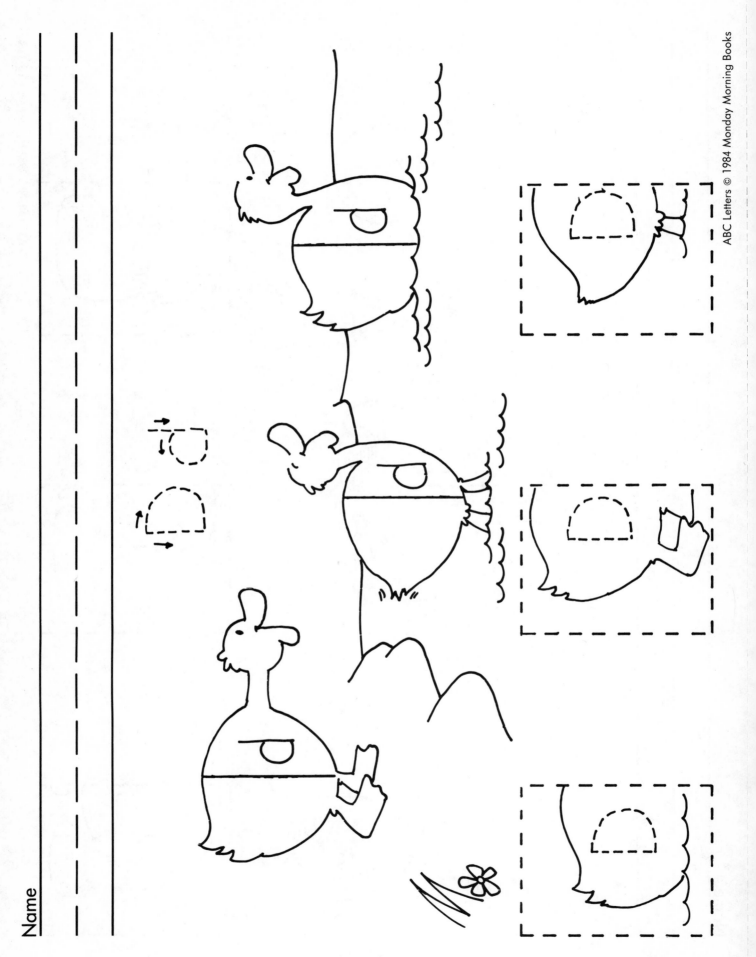

Name

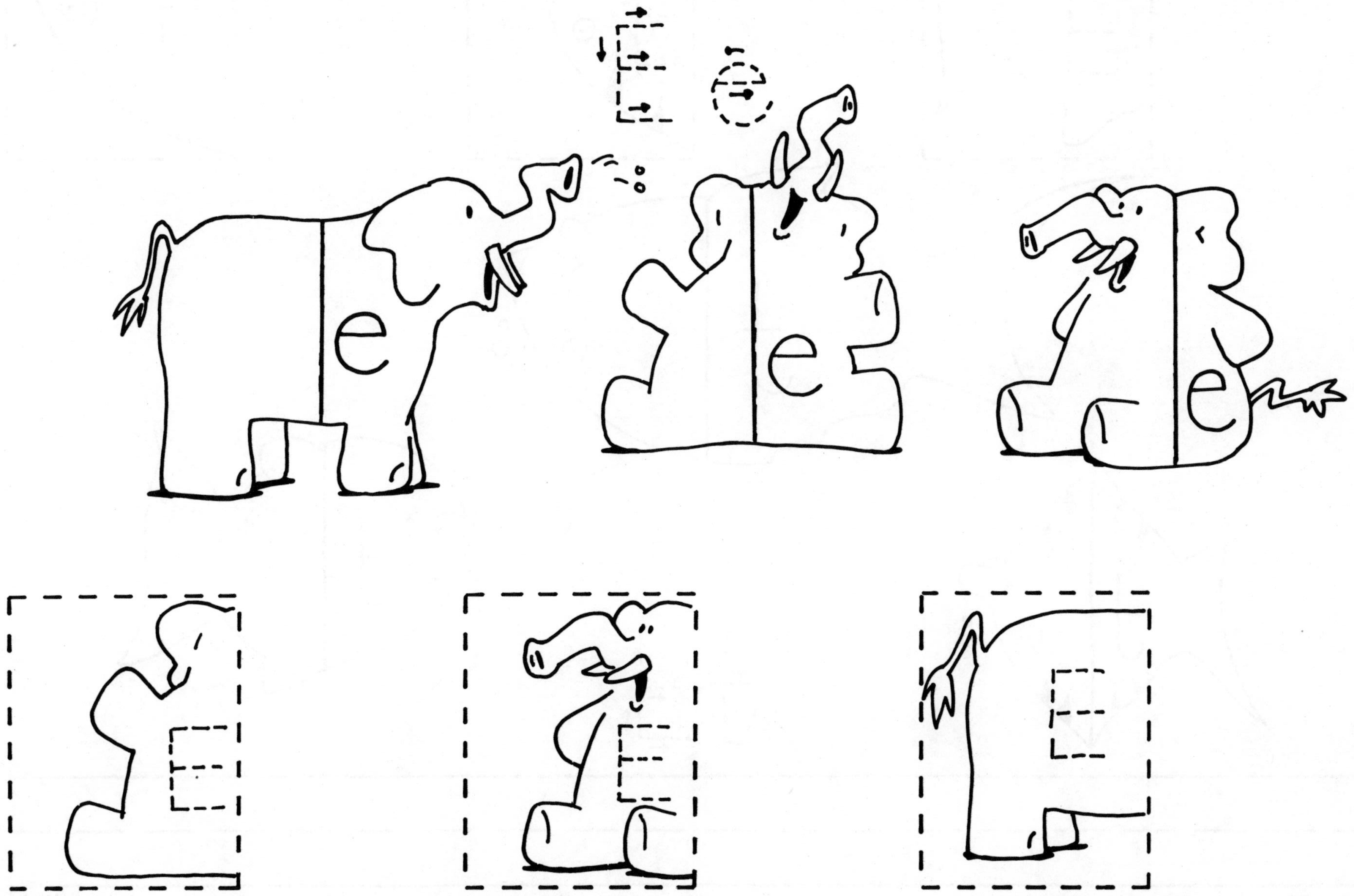

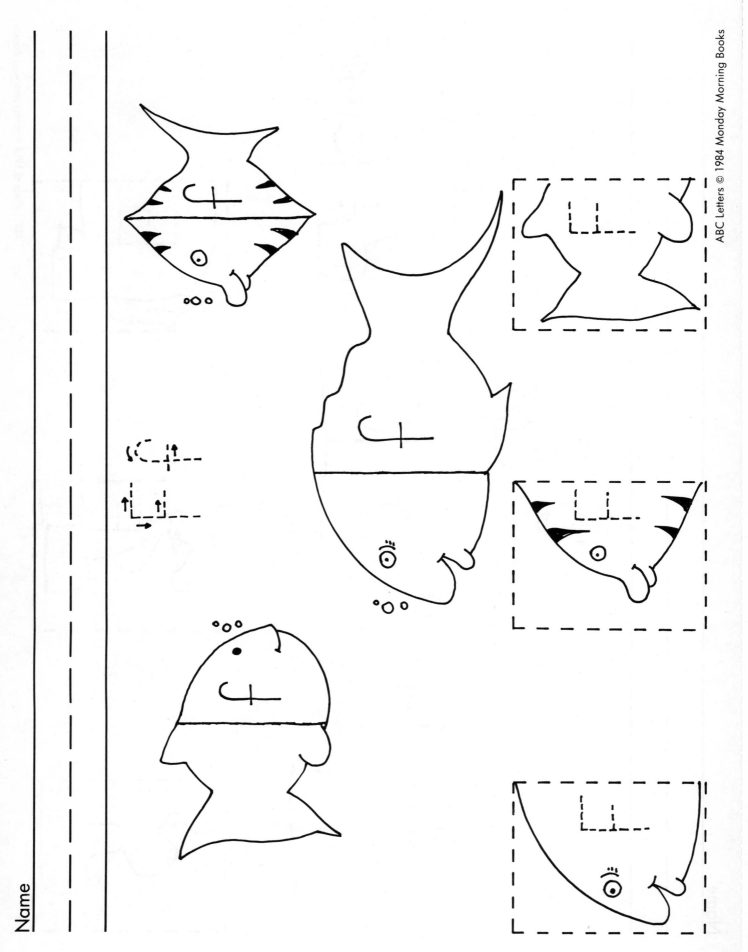

Name

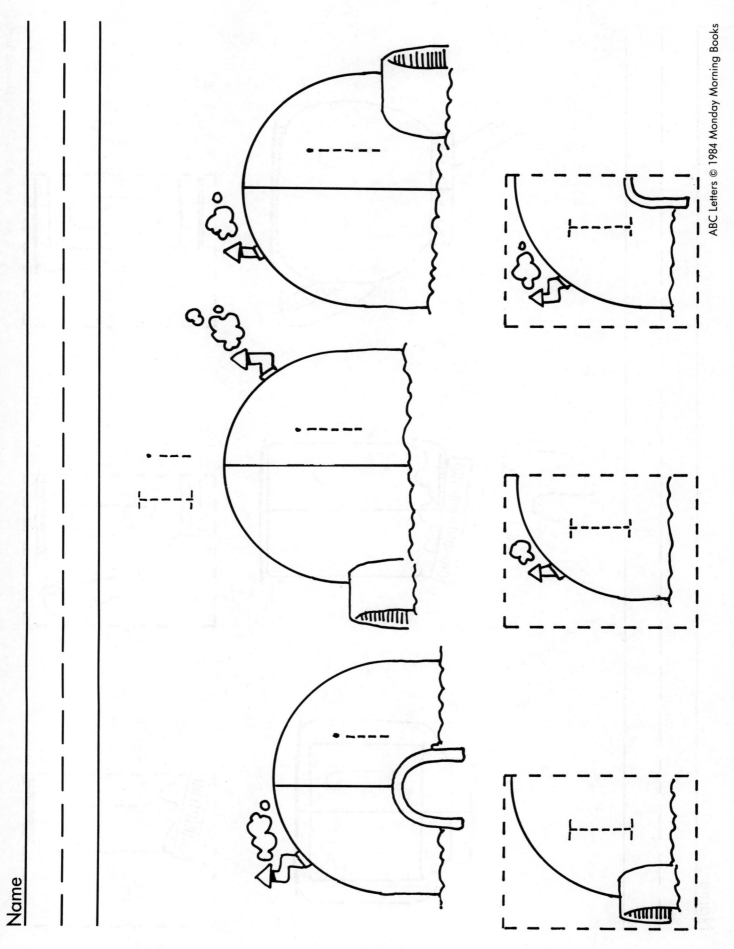

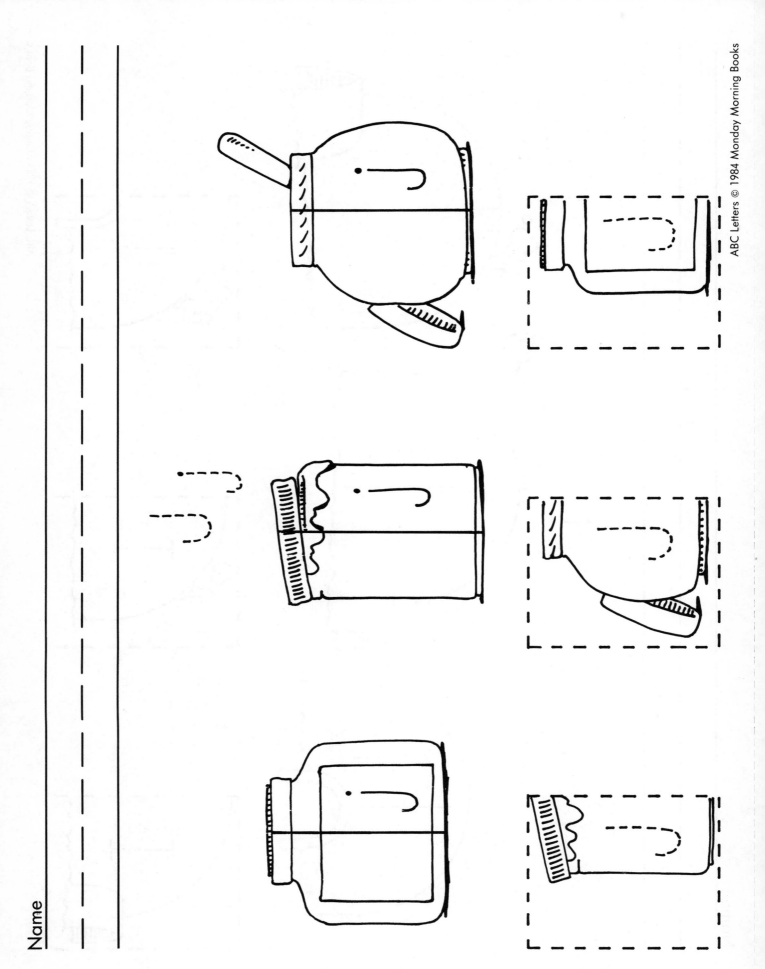

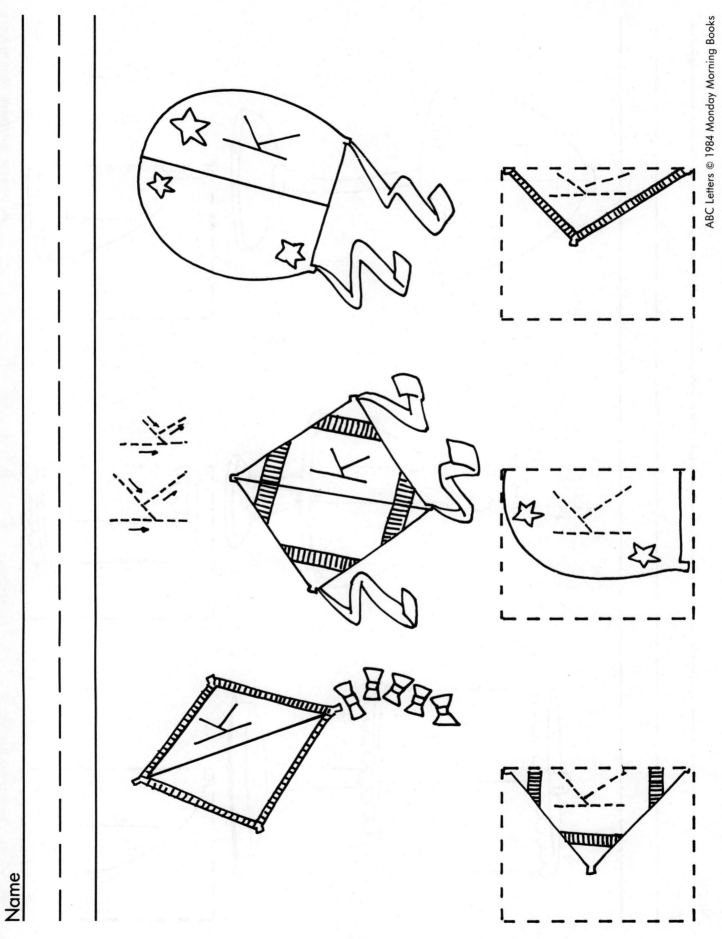

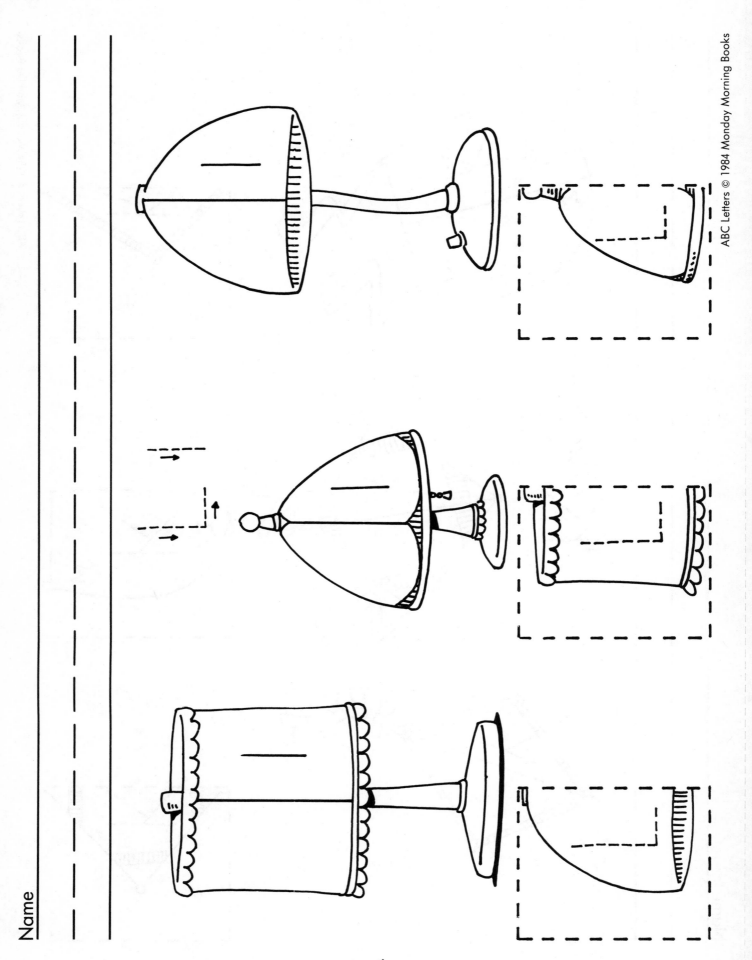

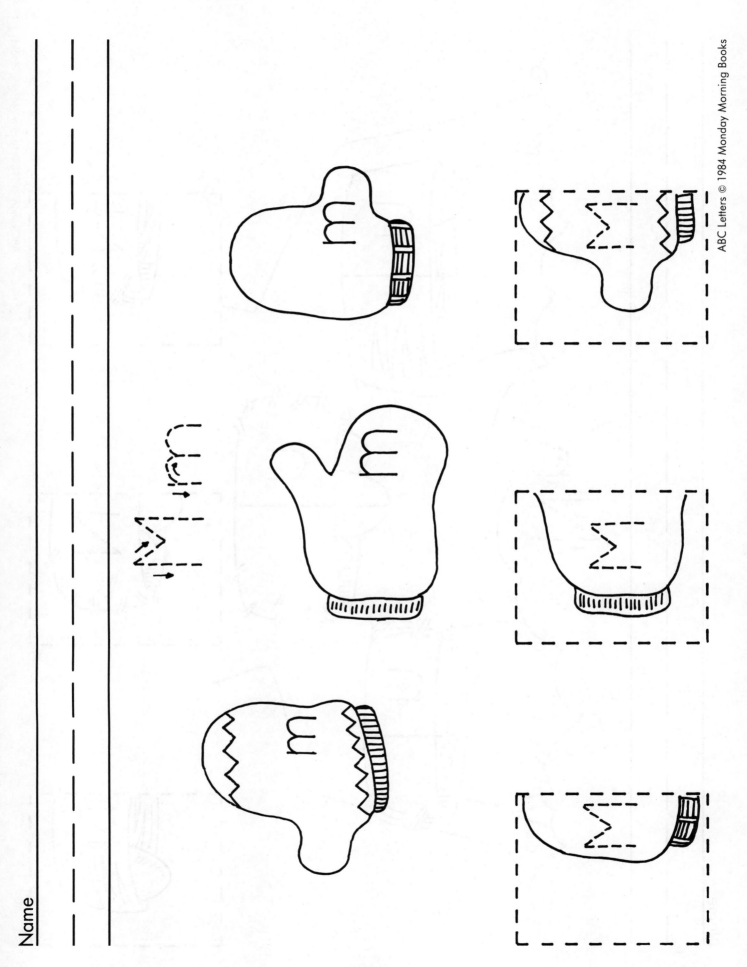

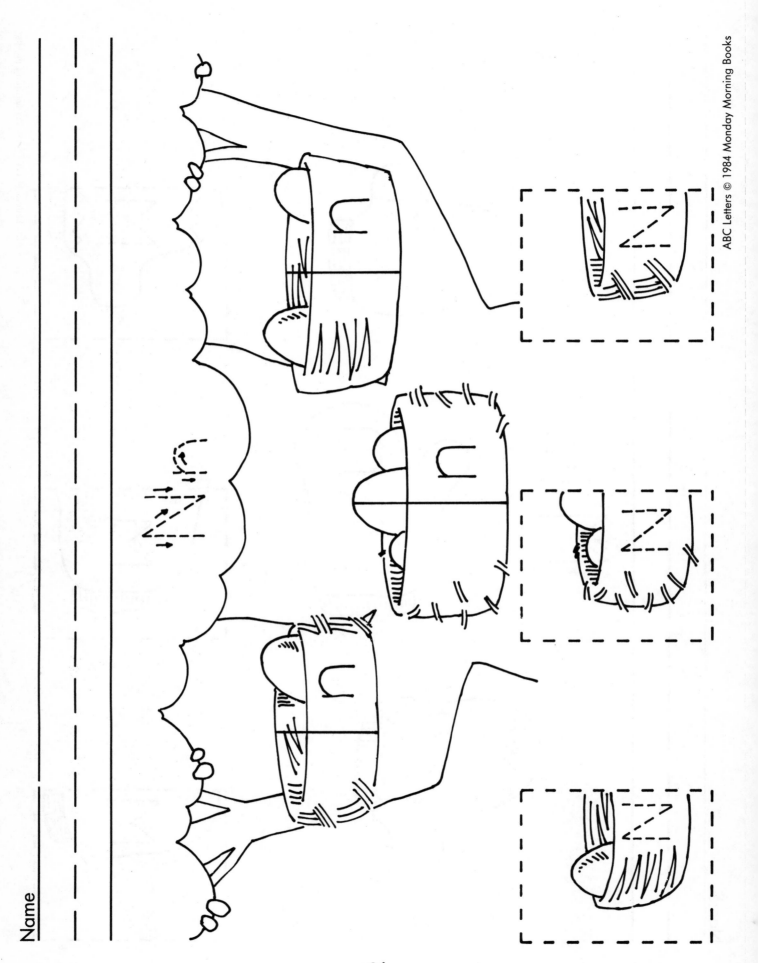

Name

Name

27

P

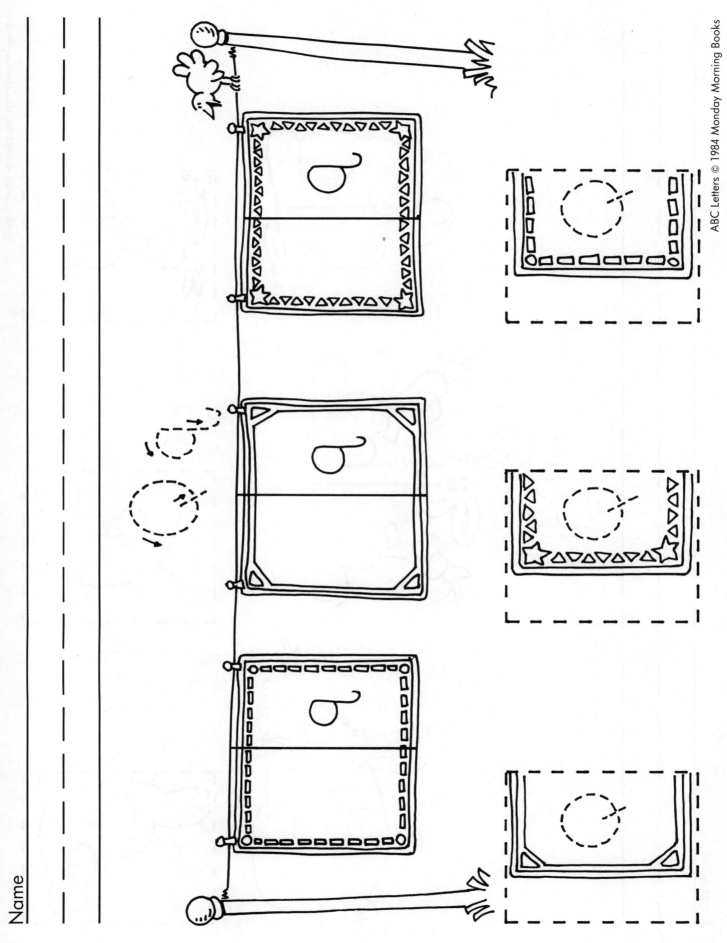

Name

30

Name

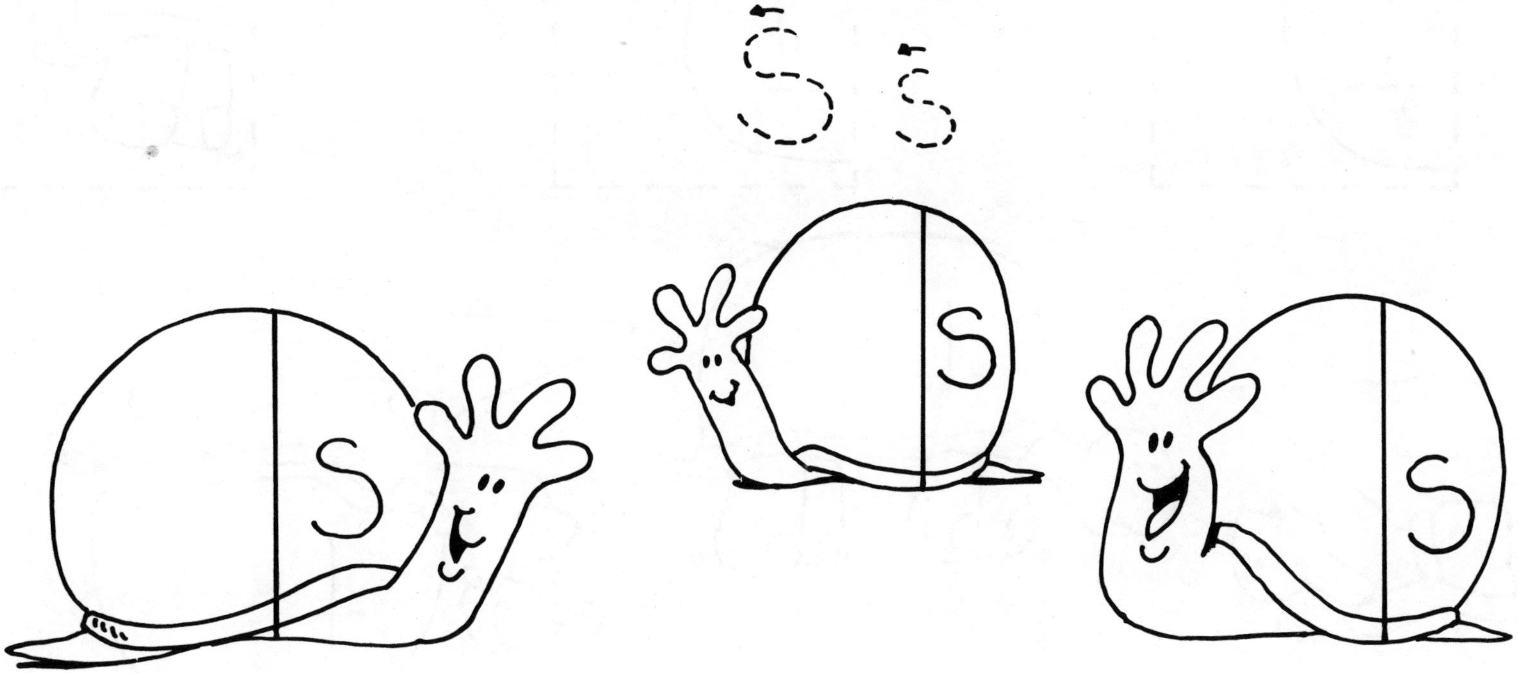

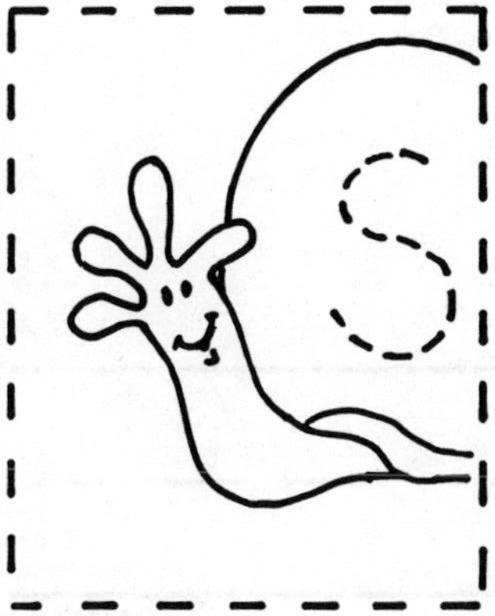

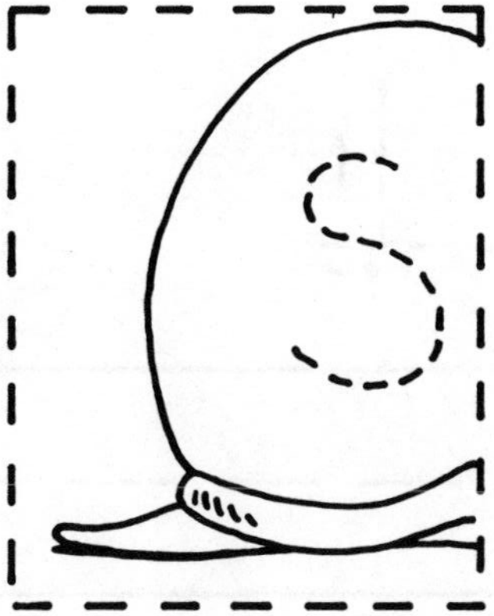

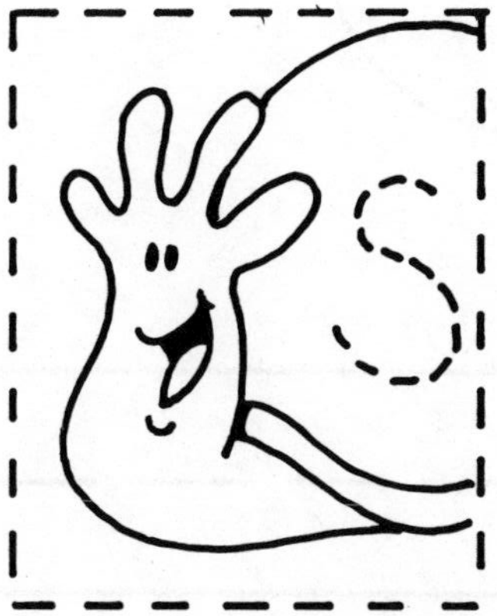

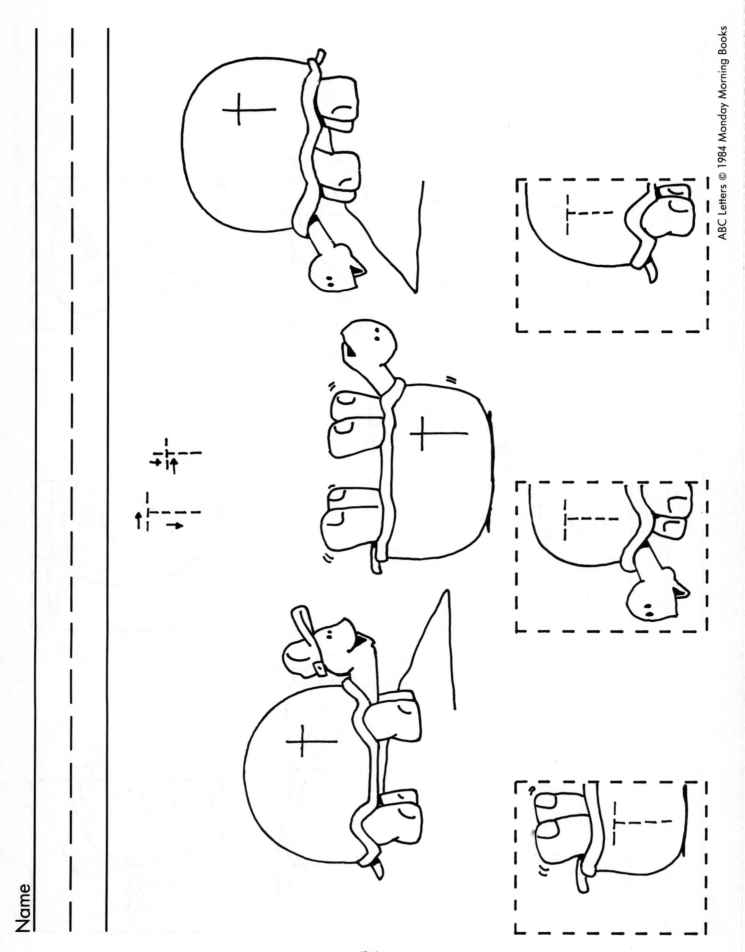

Name

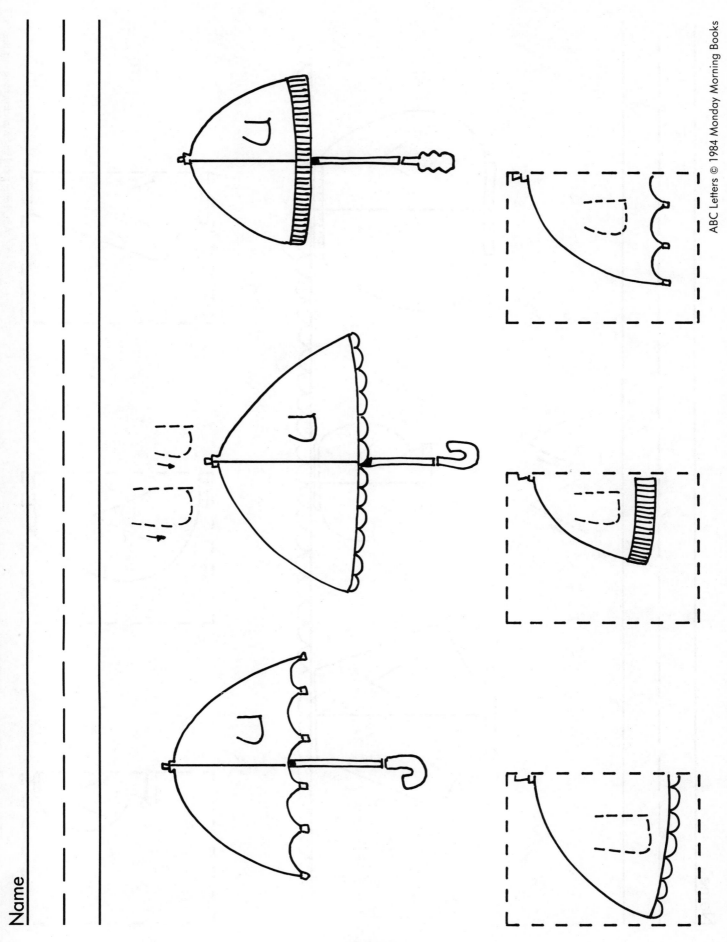

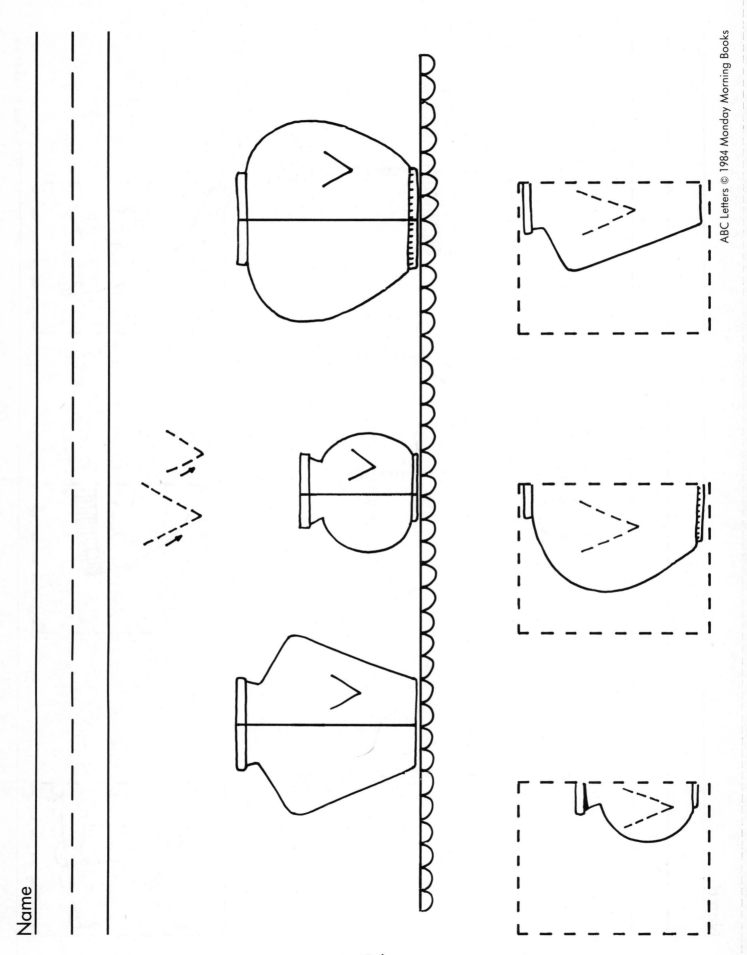

ABC Letters © 1984 Monday Morning Books

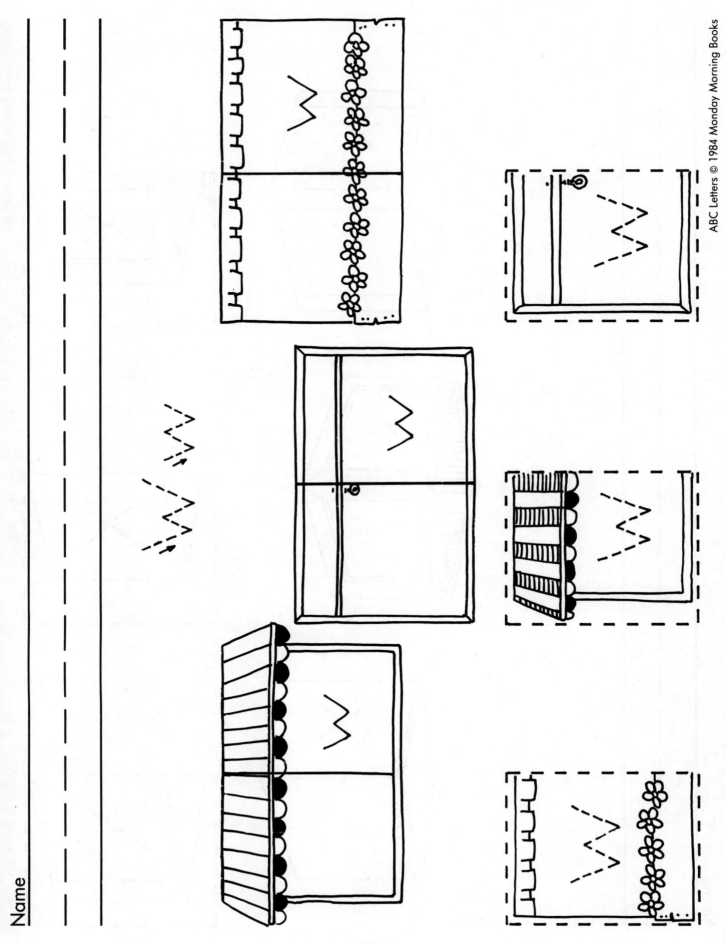

Name

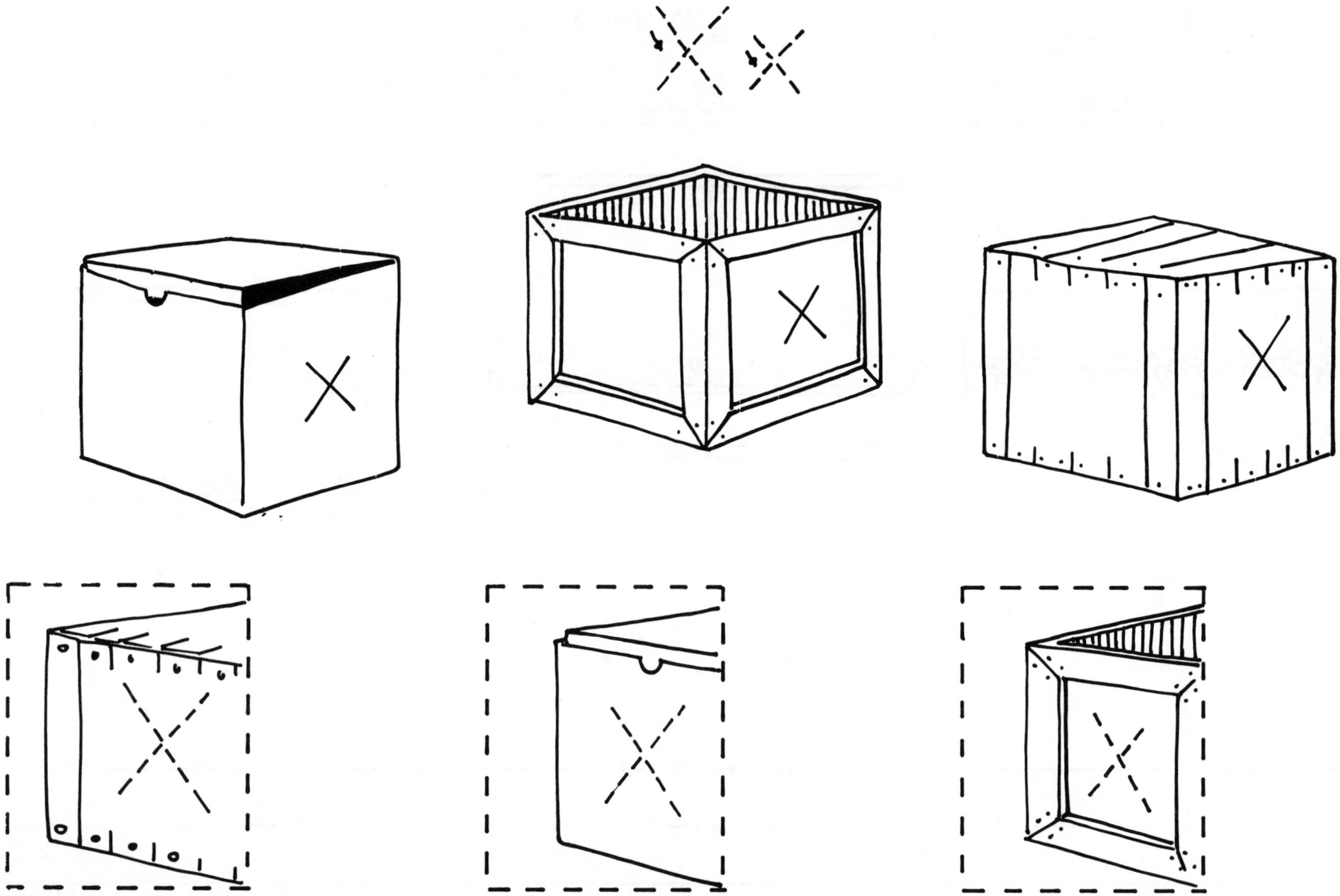

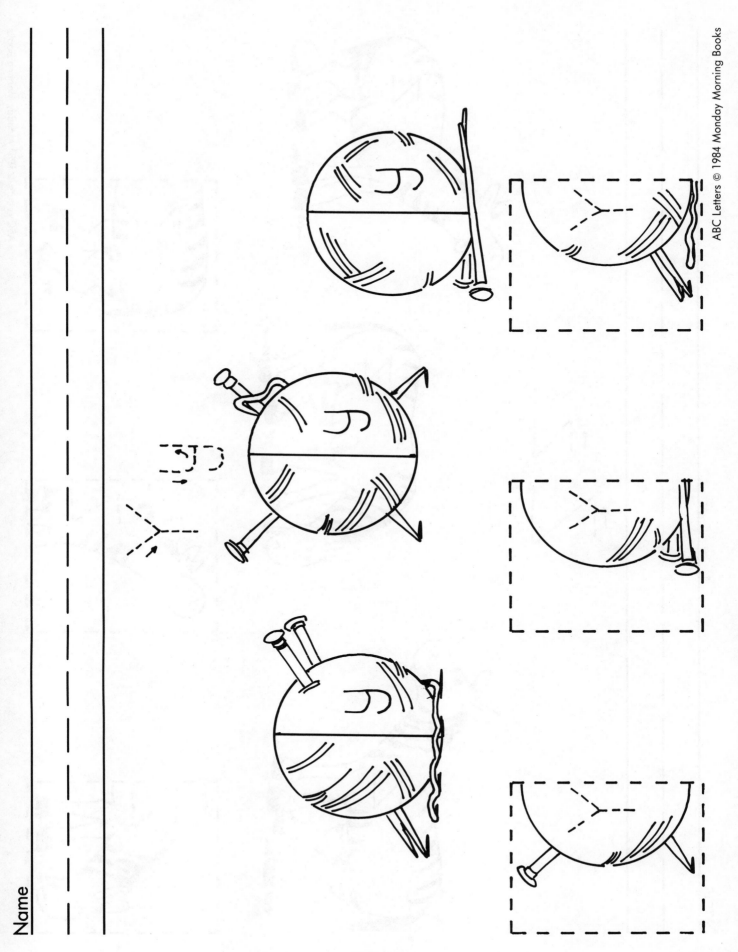

N

ABC Letters © 1984 Monday Morning Books

The worm was hungry! Find out how much of the apple he ate.
Color all the **a**'s yellow. Color the apple and the worm red.

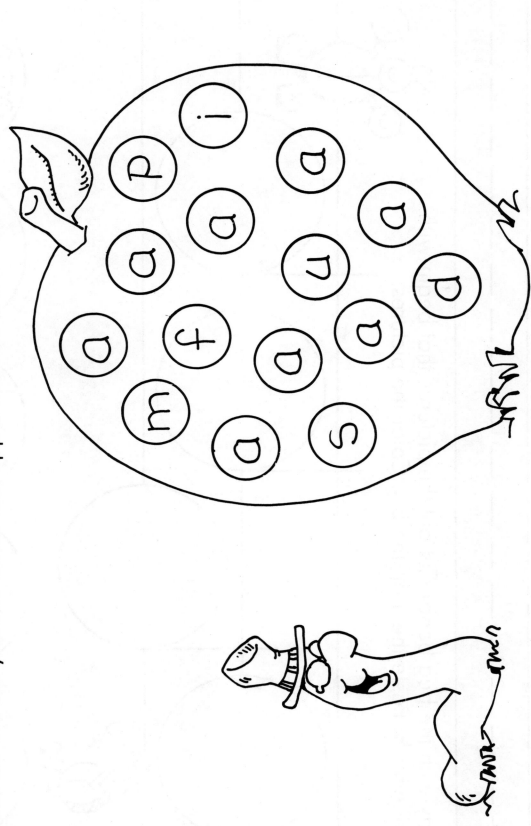

Play with the bug band! Cut out the pictures that begin with the letter **b**. Paste them on the **b**'s. Color the pictures.

These crazy cars have missing parts. Cut out the parts with the letter **c**. Paste them on the cars they match.

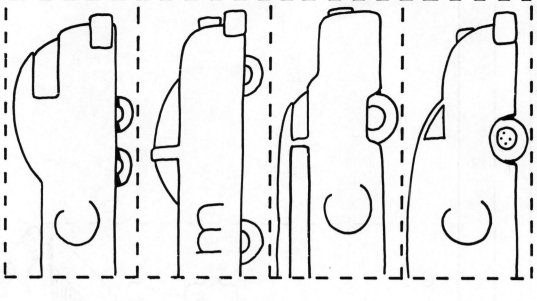

ABC Letters © 1984 Monday Morning Books

Name _____

What is behind the doors? Fold the doors, then open them.
Color the things that begin with the letter **d.**

42

Some of the eggs are missing! Cut out the eggs with the letter **e**. Paste them in the box. Color the eggs.

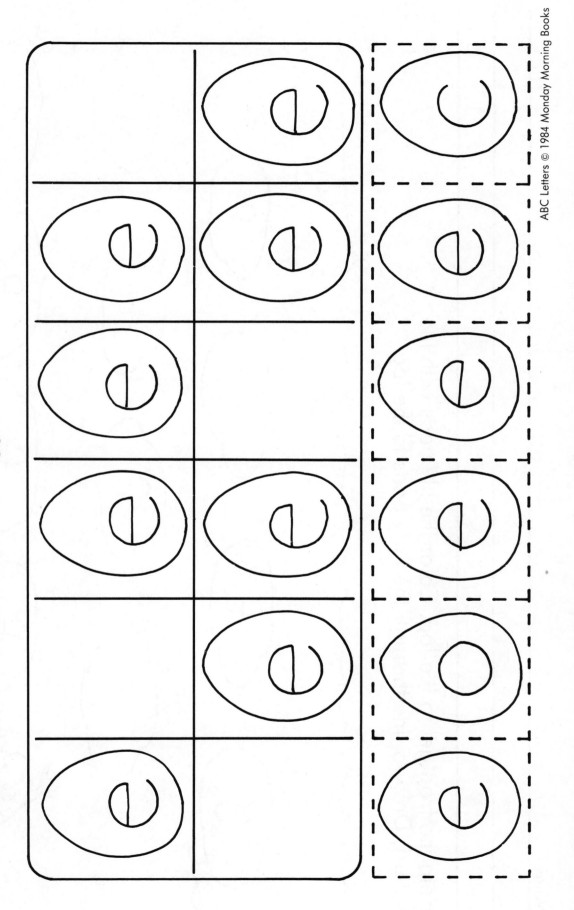

Help the frog get to the log. Color the lily pads with the letter **f**. Draw a line through the **f** lily pads to the log.

log

f

f

f

f

n

f

k

p

f

f

h

g

Name

Show the goat the way to the grass. Color the rocks with the letter **g** brown. Draw a line through the **g** rocks to the grass.

ABC Letters © 1984 Monday Morning Books

45

Cut out the pictures of things that begin with the letter **h**.
Paste them on the hearts. Color the hearts.

Help build the igloo. Cut out the ice blocks with the letter **i**.
Paste them on the igloo.

Name _____

Here is a jungle full of animals. Color all the j spaces green. Stay on the j trail to get to the hut.

STOP

Name _____

Help Captain Kidd find the keys to his treasure chest. Color the **k** spaces red. Draw what you think is in the chest.

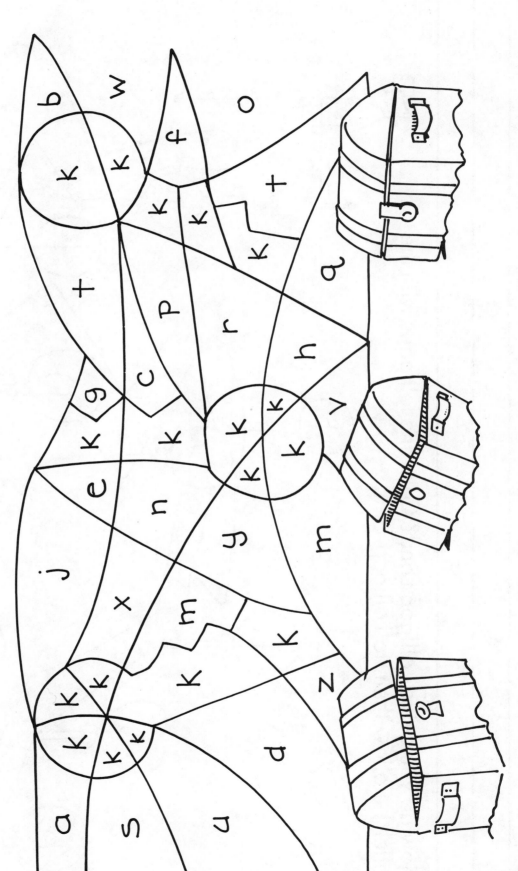

ABC Letters © 1984 Monday Morning Books

How do you get to Lollipop Land? Color the lollipops with the letter I. Follow them to Lollipop Land.

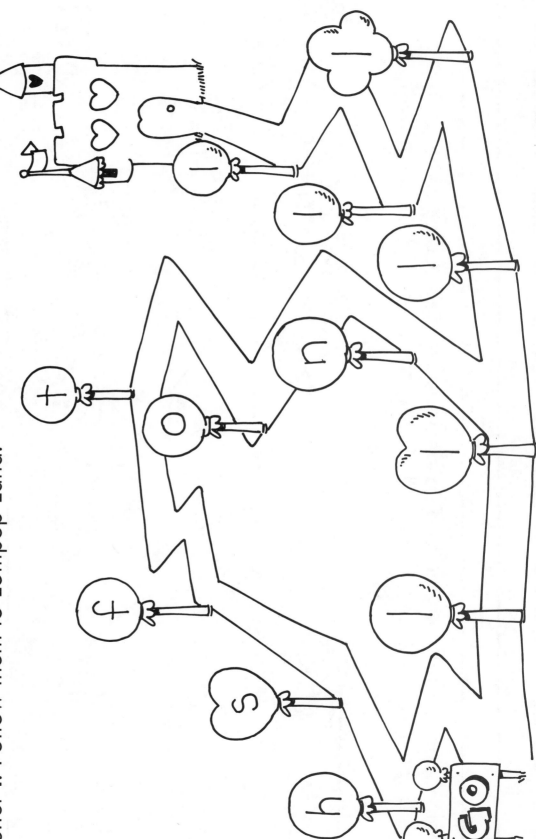

These kittens have lost their mittens. Color the mittens with
the letter **m** on them. Draw lines to show which mittens match.

Name _____

What has landed in our net? Cut out the pictures of things which begin with the letter **n.** Paste them on the net.

52

This octopus likes to blow **o**'s. Help him by drawing a ring around the letter **o**'s. Color the octopus.

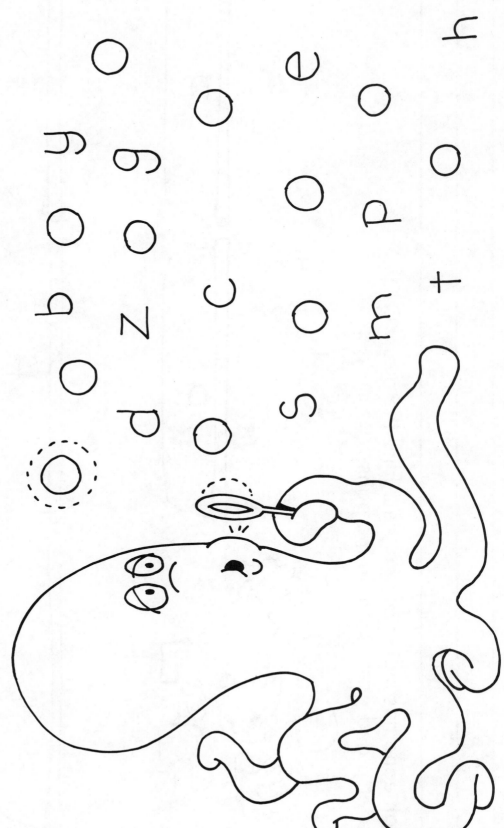

Someone has stolen all the pies! Find the pies with the letter **p** and paste them in the pans.

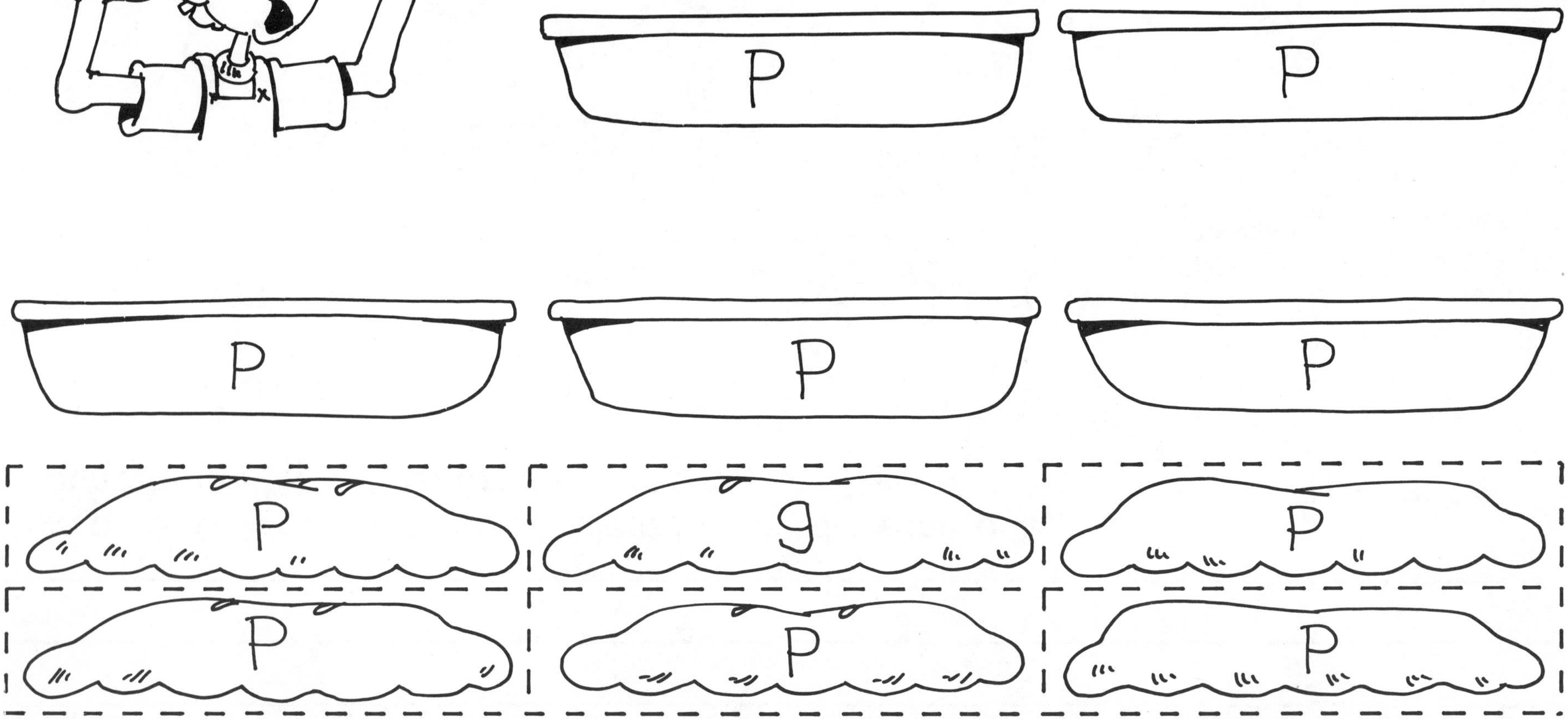

P

P

P

P

P

P

P

g

P

P

Make a patchwork quilt for the queen. Color all the patches
with the letter **q**.

Name

The rabbit has a magic **r** hat. Cut and paste all the things that begin with the letter **r**. See what he pulls from his hat.

Help the spider spin a web. Draw a line to all the letter **s**'s.
Then draw what she might catch in her web.

ABC Letters © 1984 Monday Morning Books

Fill the truck for Teddy. Cut out the pictures of things which start with the letter **t**. Paste them in the truck.

ABC Letters © 1984 Monday Morning Books

It is raining **u**'s. Circle all the letter **u**'s. Color the **u** umbrella.

59

What is in the van? Color and cut out the van. Cut out the **v** things and paste them in the van. Paste the van together.

PASTE TOGETHER

PASTE TOGETHER

VAN'S VAN

VAN'S VAN

I LOVE YOU

Help the worm clean his room. Circle the **w** things that need to be cleaned.

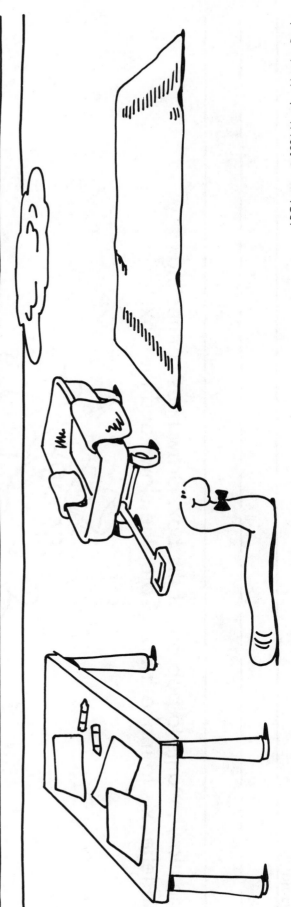

Name

The clown wants to pop out of the box. Draw lines connecting
the letter **x**'s to make a box. Color the clown and the box.

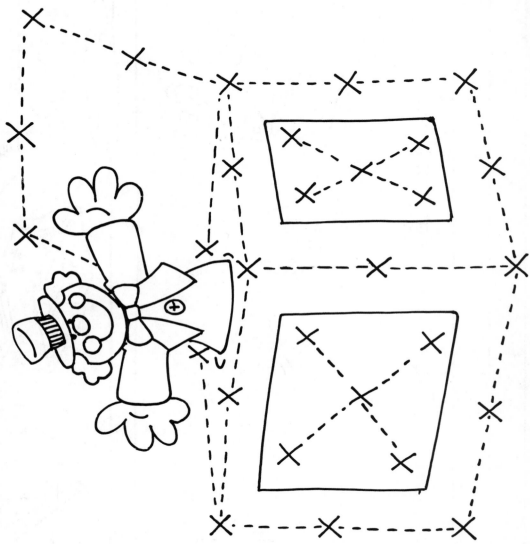

Find the letter **y**. Color all the spaces with **y**.
What do you see?

What funny animals are in this zoo! Cut out the made-up animals that begin with **z** and paste them in the zoo.

zam

zuf

pix

zat

zot

zick